The August Sleepwalker

by Bei Dao

POETRY

The August Sleepwalker (1990)
translated by Bonnie S. McDougall

SHORT STORIES

Waves (1990)
*translated by Bonnie S. McDougall
and Susette Ternent Cooke*

The
August Sleepwalker

⌣

Bei Dao

Translated and with an introduction by
Bonnie S. McDougall

A New Directions Book

Manufactured in the United States of America
New Directions books are printed on acid-free paper
Published by arrangement with Anvil Press Poetry Ltd., London; first published in the United States clothbound and as New Directions Paperbook 692 in 1990
Published simultaneously in Canada by Penguin Books Canada Limited

Library of Congress Cataloging-in-Publication Data
Pei-tao, 1949–
        [Poems. English. Selections]
        The August sleepwalker / Bei Dao ; translated and with an introduction by Bonnie S. McDougall.
            p. cm.
        Translation of: Pei-tao shih hsüan.
        ISBN 0-8112-1131-2. — ISBN 0-8112-1132-0 (pbk.)
        1. Pei-tao, 1949– —Translations, English. I. McDougall, Bonnie S., 1941– . II. Title.
PL2892.E525A25   1990
895.1'.152—dc20   89-13694
                                                                                              CIP

Acknowledgements

Forty-one of these poems were included in *Notes from the City of the Sun* edited and translated by Bonnie S. McDougall (1983, revised 1984), published as number 34 in the East Asia Papers series of the Cornell University East Asia Program.
    Nine poems ("A Toast," "You Wait for Me in the Rain," "The Host," "Rancour turns a drop of water muddy, . . ." "For Many Years," "Random Thoughts," "Notes in the Rain," "The Window on the Cliff" and "The August Sleepwalker") were first published in *Renditions* 19/20 (1983), reprinted as *Trees on the Mountain*, both published by The Chinese University Press, Hong Kong.
    Fourteen poems appeared in the *Bulletin of Concerned Asian Scholars* 16.3 (Berthoud, Colorado 1984) and in *Contemporary Chinese Literature*, ed. Michael Duke (M.E. Sharpe: Armonk, NY and London, 1985).
    We thank the editors and publishers for releasing copyright material for this edition.

New Directions Books are published for James Laughlin
by New Directions Publishing Corporation
80 Eighth Avenue, New York 10011

SECOND PRINTING

Contents

INTRODUCTION / 9
TRANSLATOR'S NOTE / 15
PREFACE TO THE AMERICAN EDITION / 16

I

Hello, Baihua Mountain / 19
Rainbow Flower / 20
I Go into the Rain Mist / 21
True / 22
Smiles, Snowflakes, Tears / 23
Cruel Hope / 24
Song of Migrating Birds / 29
A Day / 30
Notes from the City of the Sun / 31
The Answer / 33
Let's Go / 34
All / 35
Street Corner / 36
Recollection / 37
The Unfamiliar Beach / 38
A Bouquet / 40
My Transparent Grief / 41
Yes, Yesterday / 42
The Island / 43
The Witness / 46
The Bank / 47
Dusk: Dingjiatan / 48

II

Rainy Night / 51
Sleep, Valley / 52
Boat Ticket / 53
Stretch out your hands to me... / 55
The Orange Is Ripe / 56
The Red Sailboat / 57

Habit / 58
Through the melody of your breathing... / 59
You Said / 60
Our Every Morning Sun / 61
Declaration / 62
An End or a Beginning / 63
Harbour Dreams / 66
Lost / 67
Chords / 68
The Boundary / 69
Maple Leaves and Seven Stars / 70
The Old Temple / 71
In a Decade / 72
Night: Theme and Variations / 73
Tomorrow, No / 74
The Artist's Life / 75
Sequel to a Legend / 76
Love Story / 77
The Snowline / 78
Comet / 79
A Country Night / 80
Head for Winter / 81
Nightmare / 83
The Way Back / 84
A Toast / 85
You Wait for Me in the Rain / 86
Résumé / 87
Rancour turns a drop of water muddy... / 88
Accomplices / 89
Random Thoughts / 90
The Host / 92
For Many Years / 93
Portrait of a Young Poet / 94
The Echo / 96
The Window on the Cliff / 97
Strangers / 98
Notes in the Rain / 99
On Tradition / 100

III

The August Sleepwalker / 103
One Step / 104
Another Legend / 105
It has always been so... / 106
Temptation / 107
Underground Station / 108
Blanks / 109
A perpetual stranger... / 110
Orphans / 111
Bodhisattva / 112
The Art of Poetry / 113
Dirge / 114
Doubtful Things / 115
Starting from Yesterday / 116
The Fable / 117
In the Dawn's Bronze Mirror / 118
Expectation / 119
Electric Shock / 120
Language / 121
A Single Room / 122
SOS / 123
Deathwatch Night / 124
Space / 125
Don't Ask Our Ages / 126
Daydream / 127

Introduction

Bei Dao (North Island) is the pen-name of Zhao Zhenkai, one of the most gifted and controversial writers to emerge from the massive political and social upheavals of twentieth-century China. Born in Beijing in August 1949, he was just two months old when the People's Republic of China was formally inaugurated. His father was an administrative cadre in one of the non-communist parties that existed as a nominal opposition in the fifties and sixties, and his mother was a nurse, later a doctor. The family was originally from the region of Shanghai and the lower Yangtse River valley, a centre of both traditional Chinese civilization and a new modernizing culture under heavy Western influence. Bei Dao's family background reflects this double heritage, and his poetry and fiction incorporate both traditions in a natural harmony which suggests that the reconciliation of the two poses no special problem to him. The central force shaping Bei Dao's poetry has been his complex reaction to the pressures of a brutalized, conformist and corrupt society. In Beijing, the centre of government and hence also the centre of the country's hierarchical intellectual and cultural élite, from childhood on he has been familiar with its Byzantine system of rewards and punishments.

Bei Dao was educated at one of the country's top secondary schools, attended by the offspring of China's ruling class, and in the normal course of events would presumably have taken his place among them as a loyal beneficiary of the system. Normality, in the Chinese society of the fifties and early sixties, was however a fragile and unstable thing, and the Cultural Revolution which smashed all the old rules in late 1965 also brought to an end that expectation of continued cooperation between Party and intellectual élite. In his last year at secondary school, Bei Dao (like most of his generation and social class at the time) grasped the opportunity to form a new, younger and more vigorous élite as a member of the Red Guard movement. Eventually disillusioned (again like many others) with the violence and factionalism within the movement and its manipulation from above, Bei Dao abandoned direct political action and repudiated his former allegiance to authority. In the early seventies, when the violence of the Cultural Revolution had abated but its destructiveness to normal social life still continued, he became an outsider, rejecting current forms of political and social power and asserting his individuality in an apolitical mode that was ultimately subversive.

I

To Bei Dao, the world that existed around him and in his memory when he began to write was, in Nietzsche's words, "false, cruel, contradictory, misleading, senseless". To make sense of that reality, claimed Nietzsche, "we need lies in order to live". It may seem perverse to characterize Bei Dao's poetry as "lies" when it is manifestly more truthful than any of the writing that has served as literature in China since 1949. Nevertheless, to a contemporary Chinese reader, the official literature was as "real" an aspect of existence as the society that produced it, and to protest against that reality, it was necessary to discover or invent an alternative reality in an alternative literature. For reasons of both psychological and political necessity, the new literature was obliged to be "false".

Bei Dao and his fellow underground poets of the seventies created an alternative literature to challenge the orthodoxy of the entire post-1949 period. In language, imagery, syntax and structure, their poetry is highly original and obviously experimental. Scarcely less striking is the subjective and intimate voice of the love poetry and philosophical verse. But even more significant, in Bei Dao's case particularly, is the plunge into the irrational, in what was not only an extraordinary act of moral courage in the circumstances of the time, but also an act of faith in the poet's function to reveal or discover the fundamental truths of human existence. Bei Dao's early poetry is a revelation of the self inhabiting two unreal universes: a dream world of love, tranquillity and normality, that should exist but does not, and a nightmare of cruelty, terror and hatred, that should not exist but does. To depict both of these worlds, the poet was obliged to create a new poetic idiom that was simultaneously a protective camouflage and an appropriate vehicle for "un-reality."

The new writers of the seventies were in fact engaged in a search for a new poetics. The experiments in formal structure that had been a major preoccupation of Chinese modernist poets of the twenties and thirties had been more or less abandoned for many years on the Chinese mainland. Especially after 1949, poets were obliged to look to traditional idioms for inspiration—folk and classical poetry both being approved models of a broadly similar kind. The rediscovery of the Chinese past need not have been an adverse factor in the development of new forms for vernacular poetry, but the crushing weight of the literary-political establishment was inevitably inhibiting, and the "experiments" of the fifties were mechanical and conventional. The new writers of the seventies therefore picked up the threads from the thirties and forties. Unlike their predecessors, however, they did not so much try to adapt Western verse forms into Chinese but sought to find new formal devices within the general category of "free verse". This was chiefly a matter of the arrangement of ideas or imagery rather than patterns of rhyme or rhythm, though length of line, enjambement and length of verse also came under attention. Instead, their experiments centred on various kinds of oblique, oneiric imagery and elliptical syntax. The results, to some Western and Chinese eyes, strongly resemble twentieth-century modernist poetry in the West, and these poets were in fact acquainted with Western modernism. Less obviously, because of the different structure of modern written Chinese, this poetry was also similar in composition to classical Chinese verse. Conventional but dispensable grammatical forms and punctuation disappear between intensely compressed images; subject, tense and number are elusive; transitions are unclear; order and logic are supplied by the reader. The language itself is transparent enough, but there are spaces between the words and the lines whose implicit meanings are more profound than the denotative or connotative meanings of the words or lines themselves. The new poets thus achieved an exhilarating liberation from the rigidity of standard Chinese rhetoric.

II

In the eyes of the authorities, the writing of such poetry was itself an unforgivable act of political defiance, and the poets found it impossible to distance themselves from open political acts. Bei Dao took part in the Tiananmen demonstrations of spring 1976 which preceded the death of Mao Zedong and the fall of his "Gang of Four", and his most famous poem, "The Answer", is a clear expression of his personal challenge to the political leadership. Like similar poems such as "An End or a Beginning" and "Declaration", it marked his emergence from underground to dissident

11

poet. In the democratic movement of 1978-9, which pressed for further political change under the new régime of Deng Xiaoping, Bei Dao and his fellow-poet Mang Ke founded an "unofficial" literary journal, *Today*, which like the other publications of the movement was eventually banned. Over the next few years, the twists and turns of the Deng leadership in trying to balance political control with economic modernization, along with the increasingly evident corruption in all levels of party and government, produced a new wave of disillusionment among the former activists of the democratic movement. Writers like Bei Dao were drawn into the cultural bureaucracy, and were even able to publish their work in national and provincial journals, but even during the interludes of some relaxation their work was regarded officially as peripheral, while in more repressive periods Bei Dao in particular was singled out as a major target of attack.

Instead of celebrating the new post-Mao reforms, therefore, Bei Dao's work from the eighties is characterized by a new bitterness and despair. The language is much harsher, cold and clinical, and images of barrenness replace the earlier fertile symbolism of the sea and the secluded consolations of the valley. The world is now more pressing: escape, while more urgent, is less possible. Along with the increasing extinction of the poet's personality from the poems, the imagery becomes more impenetrable while the emotional force is keener. The verses are mostly short and tense, the lines abrupt and disconnected: the poet retreats further and further, leaving only the barest traces for the reader to interpret. Only in a remote and private corner are there still moments of tenderness and tranquillity, or passages of love, affection and trust.

III

In its broadest meaning, Bei Dao's poetry can certainly be called engaged, in advocating values at odds with those officially promoted. Since his work has been condemned by leading members of the literary bureaucracy, his refusal to change his style or tone is also a political act in the narrower meaning of the word. Nevertheless, on a more profound level, Bei Dao's poetry is not fundamentally an act of political engagement with the system but a statement of personal concerns that he cannot ignore or disguise. In some of the poems from the eighties there is a sense that the poet wishes he could close his eyes to the suffering around him and walk away into a private world of individual comfort, if not happiness. But along with the poet's sensibility is a stubborn honesty which refuses to deny the existence of what his sensitivity tells him. His recognition of suffering is so acute and so painful that the only way he can contain it is by transforming it into art and thereby distancing it. The so-called obscurity or bizarreness of his writing is therefore not simply adopted for reasons of expedience but is an emotional necessity dictated by an instinct for the preservation of his rationality. In other words, his verse is not obscure just because of fear of censorship but because the pain caused by all forms of oppression is so intense that conventional epithets are too shallow to express it.

This is not to suggest that Bei Dao's poetry reveals a blind sympathy with all suffering regardless of cause or kind. Beneath the imagery of the poems is a consistent philosophy that can broadly be classed as humanist: a respect for basic human needs and desires; an identification with the lost and the suffering; a belief in the dignity and responsibility of the individual; a recognition of the interconnectedness of all human beings in society; and an affirmation of the sanctity of the individual's private world. Bei Dao's poetry is above all an attempt to reveal the true nature of the self, to identify both public and private wounds, to trust in instinctive perceptions, and to reach out to other afflicted souls. To someone as intensely reserved in his personal life as Bei Dao, it would be unthinkable to carry out this search in the common coin of public rhetoric. At the same time, the intimacy of love and friendship in a society where trust can literally be a matter of life and death fostered the creation of a hermetic, semi-private language. The peculiar tensions between the density and transparency of the poems is an echo of the poet's dual commitment to revelation and communication, a paradox central to modern poetry.

Very few of Bei Dao's poems can be called happy. The most positive emotions are the appreciation of the healing powers of nature, love and companionship, and a kind of cheerfulness in the face of adversity. Knowing, as an existentialist, that the options are his, Bei Dao invests his poetry more often than not with a bleak assurance of survival against the odds. In the face of nihilism or hostility, his response to distress is to create an alternative world as witness to the perceptions of his own conscience.

Bei Dao's search for the self, therefore, holds universal meaning. His personal sense of responsibility and courage command admiration and respect, but beyond these personal qualities it is to the poetry itself that one must return as the concrete manifestation that extends beyond an individual's existence. In the poems, his private search becomes an affirmation of the universal need for and right to a world of truth and beauty. His devotion to art is not a pretended or temporary escape from society or politics but a commitment to non-political communication between people and the realization of the self.

A testimonial to the universal nature of Bei Dao's poetry is the recognition it has already won in the West, beyond the narrow circles of sinologists and political scientists. It is fair to claim that Bei Dao's poetry is translatable, since its most striking features are its powerful imagery and significant structure. The images are mostly derived from natural and urban phenomena as familiar to readers in the West as in China, not particularized as specific names of places, people or local commodities. The structures of the poems are similarly based on universal geometrical or logical patterns. The language on the whole does not rely heavily on word patterns, a particular vocabulary or special musical effects. The surface texture of the poems is therefore not significantly lost in translation, despite inevitable shortcomings. Beyond the semantic level is the question of the poems' basic concerns. Although directly inspired by the immediate problems of the author's own life and environment, they look to the core of the problems and not their outward trappings. Their interest to Western readers does not lie primarily in the political rôle they have assumed in contemporary China but in their grasp of human dilemmas present in varying degrees in all modern societies.

BONNIE S. MCDOUGALL

Translator's Note

This book is a complete translation of Bei Dao's *Collected Poems* (Bei Dao *Shi Xuan*), 2nd (expanded) edition, Canton 1987 (1st edition 1985), selected and authorized by Bei Dao himself. The collection is arranged in three parts, in chronological order, and the translation follows this arrangement. Bei Dao generally does not care to date his poems. The Western reader, however, might like to know that the poems in Part I were written between 1970 and 1978, and represent all of his early work that he wishes to acknowledge. The poems in Part II and Part III were written between 1979 and 1983 and between 1983 and 1986 respectively; they represent all the poet's published work from this time.

Forty-one of the poems in this collection were first translated in *Notes from the City of the Sun:* Poems by Bei Dao, published by Cornell University East Asia Papers in 1983, and others have appeared in journals and anthologies (see Acknowledgements). The translations have been especially revised for this edition. For a detailed analysis of the poems, see my "Bei Dao's Poetry: Revelation & Communication", in *Modern Chinese Literature* I.2 (Spring 1985) pp.225-249. For a brief account of Bei Dao's life and the controversy over his work, see the introduction to *Notes from the City of the Sun*.

The acknowledgement to *Notes from the City of the Sun* reads as follows:

In translating these poems I have on occasion departed from the literal meaning of the original when a freer rendering made a better line in English and involved no distortion of the basic meaning. Otherwise I have tried to keep close to the original, though the ambiguity in the poems leaves room for several interpretations. I am most grateful to the people who assisted me in understanding the poems, correcting the translation, advising on the introduction and arranging the publication. In particular I would like to thank Göran Malmqvist, Bai Jing, Sun Xiaobing, Anders Hansson, Annika Wirén, Carole Murray, David S.L. Goodman and Edward M. Gunn. I also wish to thank Jonathon D. Spence and Leo Ou-fan Lee for their encouragement and advice. Above all I wish to thank the author for his permission to translate and publish his poems with the original texts. I remain solely and wholly responsible for the interpretation and wording of the English translation and for the introduction. [1982]

In revising and translating additional poems for this edition, I also wish to thank Chen Maiping, Mi Qiu and Peter Jay for their constant and generous assistance.

B.McD.
June 1988

Preface to the American Edition

In the mid-1980s, when Bei Dao was travelling in Europe and America giving poetry readings and lectures, China in the eyes of most Western observers had made considerable advances along the way of economic progress, political reform, and cultural enlightenment. The poem "Daydream" (written in 1986 and the last in this collection), however, opens with images of military atrocities and skeletal petrification, and ends with the funeral of the "director of the great tragedy." The bleak despair of this poem was prophetic: the brutal suppression of the students' democratic movement in 1989 showed the promise of the 1980's to be an illusion.

In February, 1989, Bei Dao and an associate organised a petition of 33 prominent Chinese literary intellectuals to protest against the continued incarceration of one of the leaders of the 1978 democratic movement, Wei Jingsheng. Some of those who signed the petition are now believed to be under detention; several of them, including Bei Dao himself, are in involuntary exile abroad. But the hope and courage of the Tiananmen students and their supporters will not be forgotten. Bei Dao and his fellow-editors are reviving *Today,* their literary magazine from the Democracy Wall of '78. A new age of Chinese culture in exile is about to begin.

B.McD.
Oslo, October 1989

Part One

Hello, Baihua Mountain

The sound of a guitar drifts through the air,
Cupped in my hand, a snowflake quivers lightly.
Thick patches of fog draw back to reveal
A mountain range, rolling like a melody.

I have gathered the inheritance of the four seasons.
There is no sign of man in the valley.
Picked wild flowers continue to grow,
Their flowering is their time of death.

Along the path in the primordial wood
Green sunlight flows through the slits.
A russet hawk interprets into bird cries
The mountain's tale of terror.

Abruptly I cry out,
"Hello, Bai—hua—Mountain."
"Hello, my—child," comes the echo
From a distant waterfall.

It was a wind within a wind, drawing
A restless response from the land,
I whispered, and the snowflake
Drifted from my hand down the abyss.

Rainbow Flower

At the edge of the abyss
You guard my every lonely dream—
The rustle of wind through the grass.

The sun in the distance blazes brightly,
Standing by the ditch you cast a shadow,
Ripples cover the surface, sinking yesterday's time.

Should there come a day when you too must wither,
I have just a simple hope:
That you may keep the calm of your first flowering.

I Go into the Rain Mist

Dark clouds are undulating hours.
Birds scatter in all directions.
Slanting blue lines
Lash the dark trees
As if lashing a thousand canes
And a thousand old men's hearts.
—Heart, where is home,
Where is your roof?

Grass is drunk in sobbing,
Chrysanthemums imitate soberness.
Wind says to rain, You were once
Water, and to water shall return.
Then rain withdraws its first swordpoints,
And flows into streams that pour into rivers.

On the ice, silent lightning
Makes the deep banks retreat with a boom
Then close abruptly again.

True

The dense mist has painted each tree trunk white,
In the long loose hair in the stable
Wild bees whirl. Green flood water
Is just the dawn blocked off by the embankment.

On this morning
I forgot our ages.
The ice was cracking and on the water
Stones retained our fingerprints.

True, this is spring.
Pounding hearts disturb the clouds in water.
Spring has no nationality,
Clouds are citizens of the world.

Become friends again with mankind,
My song.

Smiles, Snowflakes, Tears

Everything is spinning rapidly,
Only you are smiling softly.

From the smile's red rose
I've plucked the winter's song.

O deep blue snowflakes,
What are you saying in whispers?

Give me an answer—
Are stars always stars?

Cruel Hope

1

Stirring up brown shadows
the wind has carried away the pine trees' endless chatter

The miserly night
scatters starry silver coins among the beggars
the stillness has also grown feeble
and can't stop children talking in their sleep

2

A never to be repeated night
a never to be repeated dream
sink in the silently fading morning mist

3

Two pairs of big child's eyes
hide under the gloomy eaves
the small skylight has lost its sight
and can't gather the stars that bring the frost flowers
the morning glory has been struck dumb
and can't tell fairy tales in the moonlight

We have said goodbye
to childhood friends and colourful dreams
the earth rushes on...
let the retreating horizon
collapse in a mighty howl

4

How big the world is

5

A green star flashes
on billboards pink in the dawn
hand in hand
we go forward
presenting our silhouettes to the sky

6

An airy willow catkin
soars from a tiny palm
let it fly away to reveal the secrets of the misty seas
let it fly away and ride the rough wind

7

What's that making an uproar
it seems to come from the sky

Hey, sun—kaleidoscope
start revolving
and tell us innumerable unknown dreams

8

Striking up a heavy dirge
dark clouds have lined up a funeral procession
the sun sinks towards an abyss
Newton is dead

9

Under the low eaves of heaven
a pale grey fence is woven
tiny mushrooms of bubbles
fill the roadside ditch

Drop by drop the rain
slides down our grieving cheeks

10

A shattered vase
lies embedded in brown clay

Frail reeds cry out
how can we put an end to this insane slaughter

11

Thus perhaps
we have lost
the sun and the earth
and ourselves

12

Hope
the earth's bequest
seems so heavy

silent
cold

Frost flowers drift away with the mist

13

Night
an azure net
with starlight knots

The sound of a clock telling the time

This solemn prelude
makes me believe in death

14

Dark purple waves have congealed
between the hills
under the small swaying bridge
crows circle overhead
without a sound

15

A dove flew off in haste
setting adrift a white feather

What have you inherited
child
from your mother's blood

16

Tears are salty
ah, where is the sea of life

I wish every living person
could laugh truly
and weep freely

17

In the end
even the thunder was struck dumb

Darkness
has covered up filth and evil
and blocked off pure eyes

18

A drowsy kerosene lamp
in a humble wheezy voice
describes its knowledge of another planet
with a sigh of a wisp of azure smoke
it takes down its pale blue halo

19

A golden balloon rises in the air
we hold an invisible line

Drift away
drift beyond the black ocean
towards the clear blue sky

20

The sound of a clock telling the time

What does this solemn prelude
really mean

21

Hope
the earth's bequest
seems so heavy

silent
cold

Song of Migrating Birds

We are a flock of migrating birds
Who have flown into winter's cage;
In the green early dawn we set off
On our flight to the ends of the earth.

Let our shed feathers
Fall on the heads of young women;
Let our strong wings
Bear the sun aloft.

We herd dark clouds,
Swaying manes pass through rainbows;
We herd the winds,
Flying pockets are filled with songs.

It is our cries
That frighten icebergs into ancient tears;
It is our jeers
That shame roses into crimson cheeks.

North, our homeland,
Accept our dream: let a tree
Grow from each crack in the ice
To bear great and small bells of joy . . .

A Day

Lock up your secrets with a drawer
leave notes in the margin of a favourite book
put a letter in the pillarbox and stand in silence a while
size up passers-by in the wind, without misgivings
study shop windows with flashing neon lights
insert a coin in the telephone room
cadge a smoke from the fisherman under the bridge
as the river steamer sounds its vast siren
stare at yourself through clouds of smoke
in the full-length dim mirror at the theatre entrance
and when the curtain has shut out the clamour of the sea
   of stars
leaf through faded photos and old letters in the lamplight

Notes from the City of the Sun

Life

The sun has risen too

Love

Tranquillity. The wild geese have flown
over the virgin wasteland
the old tree has toppled with a crash
acrid salty rain drifts through the air

Freedom

Torn scraps of paper
fluttering

Child

A picture enclosing the whole ocean
folds into a white crane

Girl

A shimmering rainbow
gathers brightly coloured feathers

Youth

Red waves
drown a solitary oar

Art

A million scintillating suns
appear in the shattered mirror

People

The moon is torn into gleaming grains of wheat
and sown in the honest sky and earth

Labour

Hands, encircling the earth

Fate

The child strikes the railing at random
at random the railing strikes the night

Faith

A flock of sheep spills out of the green ditch
the shepherd boy plays his monotonous pipe

Peace

In the land where the king is dead
the old rifle sprouting branches and buds
has become a cripple's cane

Motherland

Cast on a shield of bronze
she leans against a blackened museum wall

Living

A net

The Answer

Debasement is the password of the base,
Nobility the epitaph of the noble.
See how the gilded sky is covered
With the drifting twisted shadows of the dead.

The Ice Age is over now,
Why is there ice everywhere?
The Cape of Good Hope has been discovered,
Why do a thousand sails contest the Dead Sea?

I came into this world
Bringing only paper, rope, a shadow,
To proclaim before the judgement
The voice that has been judged:

Let me tell you, world,
I—do—not—believe!
If a thousand challengers lie beneath your feet,
Count me as number one thousand and one.

I don't believe the sky is blue;
I don't believe in thunder's echoes;
I don't believe that dreams are false;
I don't believe that death has no revenge.

If the sea is destined to breach the dikes
Let all the brackish water pour into my heart;
If the land is destined to rise
Let humanity choose a peak for existence again.

A new conjunction and glimmering stars
Adorn the unobstructed sky now;
They are the pictographs from five thousand years.
They are the watchful eyes of future generations.

Let's Go

Let's go—
Fallen leaves blow into deep valleys
But the song has no home to return to.

Let's go—
Moonlight on the ice
Has spilled beyond the river bed.

Let's go—
Eyes gaze at the same patch of sky
Hearts strike the twilight drum.

Let's go—
We have not lost our memories
We shall search for life's pool.

Let's go—
The road, the road
Is covered with a drift of scarlet poppies.

All

All is fate
all is cloud
all is a beginning without an end
all is a search that dies at birth
all joy lacks smiles
all sorrow lacks tears
all language is repetition
all contact a first encounter
all love is in the heart
all past is in a dream
all hope comes with footnotes
all faith comes with groans
all explosions have a momentary lull
all deaths have a lingering echo

Street Corner

The wind has dropped.
It stands at the crossing in silence.
Railings that float up in the mist,
A small door that opens at night:
Darkness proposes a toast in street lights.

The window lattice in your eyes
Filters out the hazy daylight.
Learn to leave
As you learnt everything before,
As you learnt to be glad and to grieve.

Turn and go, let the feeble
Lamplight fall on your shoulders.
Perhaps you'd like to smile, girl
But the frost netted in your braids
Trickles down with the night dew.

Recollection

Candle light
flickers on each face
leaving not a trace
the shadow's spray
strikes the white wall lightly
the guitar hanging from the wall
begins to sound in the darkness
like the masthead light reflected in water
stealing whispers

The Unfamiliar Beach

1

The sails hang down.

The masts, this wintry forest,
Have brought an unexpected hint of spring.

2

The lighthouse ruins
Mourn the departed beams.

Leaning against the remaining stairs
You strike a succession of monotonous notes
On the rusty railing.

3

Shadows choose a resting place
In the gravity of noon.
In every corner
Salt condenses the cold of the past
And the flashing light of memory.

4

In the distance
A vast expanse of white.

The horizon,
This swaying deck, how many
Slumbering nets has it cast?

5

A scarf,
The red bird,
Flies over the Sea of Japan.
The flaming reflection throws
The shadow that has left you
Towards the firmament that belongs to none.

It's enough that there isn't a storm,
But the wind is constantly shifting.
Perhaps in answer to a summons
Wings twang a cry.

6

In layer on layer
Over the golden carpet,
The ebbing tide
Disgorges the foaming night,
A loosened hawser, a broken oar.

Bending their naked bodies, fishermen
Raise the temple demolished in the storm.

7

Children chase a crescent moon.

A seagull flutters towards us
But doesn't settle on your outstretched hand.

A Bouquet

Between me and the world
You are a bay, a sail
The faithful ends of a rope
You are a fountain, a wind
A shrill childhood cry

Between me and the world
You are a picture frame, a window
A field covered with wild flowers
You are a breath, a bed
A night that keeps the stars company

Between me and the world
You are a calendar, a compass
A ray of light that slips through the gloom
You are a biographical sketch, a bookmark
A preface that comes at the end

Between me and the world
You are a gauze curtain, a mist
A lamp shining into my dreams
You are a bamboo flute, a song without words
A closed eyelid carved in stone

Between me and the world
You are a chasm, a pool
An abyss plunging down
You are a balustrade, a wall
A shield's eternal pattern

My Transparent Grief

My transparent grief
is filled with you, like green night mist
winding around a solitary shrub
but piece by piece you shred the mist
sucking the air through cold fingers
as if sucking the skin formed on milk
then you puff out a golden moon
which rises slowly and lights up the path

Yes, Yesterday

With your arm you shielded your face
And the turmoil in the forest.
Slowly you closed your eyes:
Yes, yesterday...

With berries you daubed the sunset
And your own embarrassment.
You nodded and gave a sweet smile:
Yes, yesterday...

In the darkness you struck a match
And held it between our hearts.
You bit a pallid lip:
Yes, yesterday...

A folded paper boat goes in the stream
Laden with our earliest vows.
Firmly you turned and went away:
Yes, yesterday...

The Island

1

You navigate the foggy sea
without a sail
you moor in the moonlit night
without an anchor

here fades the way
here starts the night

2

there are no signs
no clear demarcations
only the steep cliffs worshipped by the foam
retain time's oppressive traces
and a string of solemn memories

the children go down to the beach
a distant whale in the moonlight
sends a spout of water high in the air

3

the seagulls awake
wing linked with wing
their cries so sad and shrill
agitate each wattle leaf
and the children's hearts

is it only pain that is brought to life
in this tiny world

4

the horizon tilts
swinging as it tumbles down
a seagull falls
hot blood curls the broad rush leaves
the omnipresent night
covers the sound of the shot

—this is forbidden ground
the end of liberty
the quill stuck in the sand
bears a warm breath which belongs
to the tossing boat and the monsoon
to the shore and the rain's slanting threads
but the sun of yesterday or tomorrow
now writes here
the secret that death has made public

5

a gleaming feather floats
on top of every wave

the children stack small sandhills
seawater laps around them
like a garland, bleakly rocking
the moonlight's elegiac lines stretch to the end of the sky

6

ah, palm tree
it is your silence
that raises the rebel's sword
one more time
the wind lifts up your hair
like a flag to flutter in the breeze

the final boundary
rests forever in the children's hearts

7

standing against the wind
night spreads a soft carpet
and sets out rows of shell cups
for the disaster
for the hidden assassin

8

it is enough that there be a guiltless sky
it is enough that there be a sky

listen, the guitar
summons the lost sound

The Witness

As strangers, our glances
met at the crossroads
like two cups of medicinal wine clinked together
without making a sound

above our heads
the star knotted fast
was like the uneffaceable trace of a tear
between suffering and delight
then we heard the sound
of each other's glances

the dream world confirmed by reason
is as solid as
love confirmed by death
if you don't believe
it is just a disintegrating snowman

the star is the witness

The Bank

Companion to the present and the past
the bank, lifting a tall reed,
gazes in all directions
it is you
who keep watch on each wave
and the bewitching spray and stars
when the sobbing moon
strikes up an age-old shanty
it is so forlorn

I am a bank
a fishing haven
I stretch out my arms, waiting
for the needy children's little boats
to bring back a string of lamps

Dusk: Dingjiatan

Dusk, dusk
Dingjiatan is your blue shadow
dusk, dusk
your sweetheart's hair floats on your shoulder

she holds a bunch of white roses
and brushes the dust away with her lashes
it is the martyr's holy name
that freedom writes on the land

he pierces the moon with his finger
like a circle of smoke from the horizon
it is a gold engagement ring
the golden sealed lips of the girl

lips are lips
without a single word
their breath can still find in the valley
a shared echo

dusk is dusk
even if there are heavy shadows
the sunlight can still simultaneously
fall into both hearts

night closes in
night faces two pairs of eyes
here is a small patch of clear sky
here is dawn waiting to rise

Part Two

Rainy Night

While the shattered night in the flooded ditch
was rocking a new leaf
as if rocking its child to sleep
while the lamplight threaded raindrops
studded your shoulders
gleaming and rolling down
you said no
in such a resolute tone
but a smile revealed your heart's secret

With moist palms the low black clouds
kneaded your hair
kneading in the fragrance of flowers and my burning breath
our shadows lengthened in the street lights
connected each crossing each dream
catching the riddle of our happiness in their net
tears from earlier torments
soaked your handkerchief
forgotten in a pitchblack doorway

Even if tomorrow morning
the muzzle and the bleeding sun
make me surrender freedom youth and pen
I will never surrender this evening
I will never surrender you
let walls stop up my mouth
let iron bars divide my sky
as long as my heart keeps pounding the blood will ebb and
    flow
and your smile be imprinted on the crimson moon
rising each night outside my small window
recalling memories

Sleep, Valley

Sleep, valley
with blue mist quickly cover the sky
and the wild lilies' pale eyes
Sleep, valley
with rainsteps quickly chase away the wind
and the anxious cries of the cuckoo

Sleep, valley
here we hide
as if in a thousand-year dream
time no longer glides past blades of grass
stopped behind layers of clouds, the sun's clock
no longer swings down evening glow or dawn

Spinning trees
toss down countless hard pine cones
protecting two lines of footprints
our childhoods walked with the seasons
along this winding path
and pollen drenched the brambles

Ah, it's so quiet and still
the cast stone has no echo
perhaps you are searching for something
—from heart to heart
a rainbow rises in silence
—from eye to eye

Sleep, valley
sleep, wind
valley, asleep in blue mist
wind, asleep in our hands

Boat Ticket

He doesn't have a boat ticket
how can he go on board
the clanking of the anchor chain
disturbs the night here

the sea, the sea
the island that rises from the ebbing tide
as lonely as a heart
lacks the soft shadows of bushes
and chimney smoke
the mast that flashes lightning
is struck into fragments by lightning
innumerable storms
have left behind fixed patterns
on rigid scales and shells
and the small umbrellas of jellyfish
an ancient tale
is handed on by the ocean spray from wave to wave

he doesn't have a boat ticket

the sea, the sea
the lichen tightly massed on the reef
spreads towards the naked midnight
along the seagulls' feathers gleaming in the dark
and clings to the surface of the moon
the tide has fallen silent
conch and mermaid begin to sing

he doesn't have a boat ticket

time hasn't come to a stop
in the sunken boat the fire is being stoked
rekindling red coral flames

when the waves tower up
glittering indeterminately, the eyes of the dead
float up from the ocean depths

he doesn't have a boat ticket

yes it makes you dizzy
the sunlight drying out on the beach
makes you so terribly dizzy

he doesn't have a boat ticket

Stretch out your hands to me...

Stretch out your hands to me
don't let the world blocked by my shoulder
disturb you any longer
if love is not forgotten
hardship leaves no memory
remember what I say
not everything will pass
if there is only one last aspen
standing tall at the end of the road
like a gravestone without an epitaph
the falling leaves will also speak
fading paling as they tumble
slowly they freeze over
holding our heavy footprints
of course no one knows tomorrow
tomorrow begins from another dawn
when we will be fast asleep

The Orange Is Ripe

The orange is ripe
the sun-filled orange is ripe

Let me into your heart
heavily laden with love

The orange is ripe
its skin exudes a fine mist

Let me into your heart
grief becomes a fountain of joy

The orange is ripe
a bitter net contains each segment

Let me into your heart
to find my shattered dream

The orange is ripe
the sun-filled orange is ripe

The Red Sailboat

Ruined walls broken ramparts all around
how can the road extend beneath our feet
not morning stars but street lights that have slid
into your pupils pour forth
I don't want to comfort you
the trembling maple leaf
is scrawled with spring lies
the sunbird from the tropics
hasn't perched on our trees
and the forest fire behind
is only sunset in a cloud of dust

If the earth is sealed in ice
let us face the warm current
and head for the sea
if the reef is our future image
let us face the sea
and head for the setting sun
no, longing for a conflagration
is longing to turn into ash
but we seek only a calm voyage
you with your long floating hair
I with my arms raised high

Habit

I'm used to how you light my cigarette in the dark
as the flame quivers you always ask softly
guess what I've burned

I'm used to how you sit in the boat humming
as oars dripping water fragment the sun in the mist
how trailing weary, stubborn footsteps
you decline to rewarm our old dreams on the bench
how you race me, hair swinging from side to side
laughing freely as our shoulders part

I'm used to how you call out in the valley
listening afterwards for the echo that chases our names
how you bring your books, always asking questions
with pursed lips writing the answer on your hand
how your warm breath wraps round my neck like a scarf
under the deep blue street lights in winter

Yes, I'm used to
how you strike the flint that burns
the dark I'm used to

Through the melody of your breathing...

Through the melody of your breathing
I ask the night
to put the past in a porcelain vase
then the petals fold
a withered leaf
falls on the open book
dust drifts slowly upwards

I leave quietly
taking the book
with a page of you in it
your curse
your love
have both become flames in a mirror
disappearing into another
even lonelier world

A bunch of keys
sings in the still lane
don't turn around
don't look in the window that sinks in the night mist
behind the curtain a dream
clamours
through wave-like hair

You Said

Using a secret sign I knocked on the door
You said Come in spring
I slowly took off my cap
My temples drenched with frost and snow

When I held you
You said Don't be alarmed, silly
A frightened fawn
Leaping in your eyes

On your birthday
You said Don't give me a present
But my Cassiopeia
Already gleamed over your head

At the street corner
You said Don't leave, ever
A row of snow-white headlights
Passed between us

Our Every Morning Sun

The young plants' tender arms hold up the sun
Converging into a beam of light, people of different
    skin-colour
Go to you, as like a striking clock
You shake down snowdrifts from the mountain top
Fear and grief that tremble in the wrinkles' folds
Hearts no longer hide behind curtains
Books open windows and let birds fly out freely
Ancient trees no longer snore no longer bind
The children's nimble legs with withered vines
Young women return from bathing
Trailing stars and a broad moonbeam
All of us have our own names
Our own voices, loves and longings

The iceberg in a nightmare
Melts in the early morning, while from the lingering night
We lead our shadows away
May the heavy memories underfoot
Gradually disperse as we journey
Along the horizon of hands joined to hands
Every story has a new beginning
So let's begin

Declaration

for Yu Luoke

Perhaps the final hour is come
I have left no testament
Only a pen, for my mother
I am no hero
In an age without heroes
I just want to be a man

The still horizon
Divides the ranks of the living and the dead
I can only choose the sky
I will not kneel on the ground
Allowing the executioners to look tall
The better to obstruct the wind of freedom

From star-like bullet holes shall flow
A blood-red dawn

An End or a Beginning

for Yu Luoke

Here I stand
Replacing another, who has been murdered
So that each time the sun rises
A heavy shadow, like a road
Shall run across the land

A sorrowing mist
Covers the uneven patchwork of roofs
Between one house and another
Chimneys spout ashy crowds
Warmth effuses from gleaming trees
Lingering on the wretched cigarette stubs
Low black clouds arise
From every tired hand

In the name of the sun
Darkness plunders openly
Silence is still the story of the East
People on age-old frescoes
Silently live forever
Silently die and are gone

Ah, my beloved land
Why don't you sing any more
Can it be true that even the ropes of the Yellow River
    towmen
Like sundered lute-strings
Reverberate no more
True that time, this dark mirror
Has also turned its back on you forever
Leaving only stars and drifting clouds behind

I look for you
In every dream

Every foggy night or morning
I look for spring and apple trees
Every wisp of breeze stirred up by honey bees
I look for the seashore's ebb and flow
The seagulls formed from sunlight on the waves
I look for the stories built into the wall
Your forgotten name and mine

If fresh blood could make you fertile
The ripened fruit
On tomorrow's branches
Would bear my colour

I must admit
That I trembled
In the death-white chilly light
Who wants to be a meteorite
Or a martyr's ice-cold statue
Watching the unextinguished fire of youth
Pass into another's hand
Even if doves alight on its shoulder
It can't feel their bodies' warmth and breath
They preen their wings
And quickly fly away

I am a man
I need love
I long to pass each tranquil dusk
Under my love's eyes
Waiting in the cradle's rocking
For the child's first cry
On the grass and fallen leaves
On every sincere gaze
I write poems of life
This universal longing
Has now become the whole cost of being a man

I have lied many times
In my life
But I have always honestly kept to
The promise I made as a child
So that the world which cannot tolerate
A child's heart
Has still not forgiven me

Here I stand
Replacing another, who has been murdered
I have no other choice
And where I fall
Another will stand
A wind rests on my shoulders
Stars glimmer in the wind

Perhaps one day
The sun will become a withered wreath
To hang before
The growing forest of gravestones
Of each unsubmitting fighter
Black crows the night's tatters
Flock thick around

AUTHOR'S NOTE: The first draft of this poem was written in
1975. Some good friends of mine fought side by side with Yu
Luoke, and two of them were thrown into prison where they lan-
guished for three years. This poem records our tragic and indig-
nant protest in that tragic and indignant period.

Harbour Dreams

When moonlight pours into the harbour
the night air seems transparent
step by step the worn stone stairs
lead to the sky
lead to my dreams

I returned to my native town
bringing back coral and salt for my mother
the coral grew into a forest
the salt melted the ice
girls' quivering lashes
shed ripened grains of wheat
a moist wind blew
past the cliffs' decrepit foreheads
when my love song
paid a call at every window
beer foam spilled over the road
turning into a row of street lights
I walked towards the horizon glowing in the sunset
and turned around
to make a deep bow

The sea spray washed the deck and the sky
the stars searched for their daylight positions
on the compass
true I'm not a sailor
not born to be a sailor
but I'll hang my heart on the side of the ship
like an anchor
and set sail with the crew

Lost

Following the pigeon's whistle
I searched for you
the tall forest blocked off the sky
on the small path
a lost dandelion
led me to the blue-grey lake
in the gently rocking reflections
I found your
unfathomably deep eyes

Chords

The trees and I
formed a close circle round the pond
my hand dipping into the water
disturbed the swifts from sleep
the wind was all alone
the sea very far away

I walked into the streets
noise stopped behind a red light
my shadow opened like a fan
footprints askew and crooked
the safety island all alone
the sea very far away

A blue window gleamed
boys downstairs
strummed guitars and sang
cigarette ends glowed and darkened
the stray cat all alone
the sea very far away

As you slept on the beach
the wind paused by your mouth
waves surging up in silence
converged in a gentle curve
the dream was all alone
the sea very far away

The Boundary

I want to go to the other bank

The river water alters the sky's colour
and alters me
I am in the current
my shadow stands by the river bank
like a tree struck by lightning

I want to go to the other bank

In the trees on the other bank
a solitary startled wood pigeon
flies towards me

Maple Leaves and Seven Stars

The world is as small as a street scene
when we met you nodded briefly
dispensing with the past
and friendly greetings
happiness is just a passage perhaps
and all is at an end
but why do you still wear that red scarf
look, through the lace of maple leaves the sky
is very clear, and the sun
has shifted to the last windowpane

The seven stars ascending
behind the massive roofs
no longer look like a cluster of ripe grapes
it is another autumn
the street lights will soon be lit of course
I should dearly like to see your smile
forgiving but indifferent
and that calm gaze
the street lights will soon be lit

The Old Temple

Fading chimes
form cobwebs
             spreading annual rings
in splintered columns
without memories
             a stone
spreads an echo through the misty valley
a stone
             without memories
when a small path wound its way here
the dragons and strange birds flew away
carrying off the mute bells under the eaves
once a year indifferently
weeds grow not caring
whether the master they submit to is
a monk's cloth shoe
             or wind
the stele is chipped, the inscription worn away
as if only in a general conflagration
could it be deciphered
             yet perhaps
with a glance from the living
the tortoise might come back to life in the earth
and crawl over the threshold
             bearing its heavy secret

In a Decade

Over the forgotten land
the years entangled with the horse's yoke bells
rang throughout the night, and the road's panting
under the swaying load changed into a song
passed on by people everywhere
to the sound of an incantation a woman's necklace
rose into the night sky as if in affirmation
the fluorescent dial struck licentiously at will
time is as honest as a wrought-iron fence
except for the wind trimmed by withered branches
no one can pass over it or come and go
flowers that have only bloomed in books
eternally imprisoned become the mistress of truth
but yesterday's broken lamp
is so resplendent in the hearts of the blind
right up until the time when they are shot
a final portrait of the assassin is left behind
in eyes that have suddenly opened

Night: Theme and Variations

Here the roads converge
parallel beams of light
are a longwinded but abruptly interrupted dialogue
suffused with the drivers' pungent smoke
and rough muttered curses
railings have replaced the queues
the lamplight seeping out from between cracks in the
    doorboards
is cast with the cigarette butts onto the roadside
for nimble feet to tread on
an old man's forgotten walking stick against a billboard
looks as if it were ready to go
the stone waterlily has withered
in the fountain tall buildings slowly topple
the rising moon suddenly strikes
the hour again and again
arousing ancient Time inside the palace wall
the sundial calibrates errors as it turns
waiting for the grand rite of the dawn
brocade dress ribbons stand up rustling in the wind
brushing away the dust from the stone steps
the shadow of a tramp slinks past the wall
red and green neon lights blaze for him
and keep him from sleeping all night
a lost cat scurries up a bench
gazing down at the smoke-soft gleam of the waves
but the mercury vapour-lamp rudely opening the curtain
to peer at the secrets that others store
disturbs the dream wakens the lonely
behind a small door
a hand gently draws the catch
as if pulling a rifle bolt

Tomorrow, No

This is not a farewell
because we have never met
though shadow and shadow
have overlain on the street
like a solitary convict on the run

tomorrow, no
tomorrow is not the other side of night
whoever has hopes is a criminal
let the story that took place at night
end in the night

The Artist's Life

Go and buy a radish
—mother said
hey, mind the safety line
—the cop said
ocean, where are you
—the drunk said
why have all the street lights exploded
—I said
a blind man passing by
nimbly raised his cane
like pulling out an antenna
an ambulance arriving with a screech
took me to hospital

and so I became a model patient
sneezing loud and clear
closing my eyes to figure out the mealtimes
donating blood to bedbugs
with no time to sigh
in the end I was taken on as a doctor too
holding a thick hypodermic
I pace up and down in the corridor
to while the evenings away

Sequel to a Legend

There is already a legend about us
on the ancient urn
but you still keep on asking
if it is worth it
of course fire can be extinguished by the wind
and a mountain peak might fall down at dawn
and melt into a funereal night's river
the bitter fruits of love
will drop when they ripen
here and now
as long as we have the setting sun to crown us
everything that follows after
counts for nothing
—the endless night
a moment of tossing and silence

Love Story

It was only one world after all
that readied a ripe summer for us
but we continued childish games
according to the rules of grown men
not caring about those who fell by the wayside
nor for ships that ran aground

yet the sunshine that blesses lovers
casts a black and weary night
upon the backs of toilers
and even on the small path where we meet
ice and frost may fall
as we encounter hostile glances

it's no longer a simple story
in this story
there are you and I and many others

The Snowline

Forget what I've said
forget the bird shot down from the sky
forget the reefs
let them sink once more into the deep
forget even the sun
only a lamp covered in dust and ashes
is shining
in that eternal position

after a series of avalanches
the cliffs above the snowline
seal everything in silence
from gentle grassy shores
below the snowline
a stream trickles

Comet

Come back or leave forever
don't stand like that at the door
like a statue made of stone
discussing everything between us
with a look that expects no answer

in fact what is hard to imagine
is not darkness but dawn
how long will the lamplight last
perhaps a comet may appear
trailing debris from the ruins
and a list of failures
letting them glitter, burn up and turn into ash

come back, and we'll rebuild our home
or leave forever, like a comet
sparkling and cold like frost
discarding the dark, and sinking back into darkness again
going through the white corridor connecting two evenings
in the valley where echoes arise on all sides
you sing alone

A Country Night

Evening sunshine and distant hills
fold into a crescent moon
passing through an elm wood
the bird's nest is empty
a path encircles the pond
chasing a dog with a dirty coat
up to the mud wall at the village entrance
the bucket in the well sways gently
the clock is as still
as the roller in the yard
dried wheat stalks stir uneasily
the sound of chewing from the stable
is full of threat
a man's long shadow
slips down from the doorstep
firelight from a kitchen range
casts a ruddy glow on a woman's arms
and a chipped earthenware bowl

Head for Winter

The wind has blown away towards the setting sun
the sparrow's last remaining warmth

Head for winter
we weren't born for the sake of
a sacred prophecy, let's go
past the arched doorway formed by humpbacked old men
leaving the key behind
past the main hall where ghost shadows flicker
leaving the nightmare behind
leaving all our superfluous things behind
we lack for nothing
sell off even clothes and shoes
and our last rations
leaving our jingling change behind

Head for winter
singing a song
no blessings, no prayers
we will never go back
to decorate the painted green leaves
in a season that has lost its enchantment
fruit that cannot make wine
won't turn into vinegar either
roll a cigarette out of newspaper
and let the black cloud faithful as a dog
close at our heels as a dog
wipe away all the lies under the sun

Head for winter
and don't sink into green
dissipation, at ease everywhere
don't repeat the incantation of thunder and lightning
letting ellipses in thinking become streams of raindrops

or walk down the street like a prisoner
under noon's supervision
ruthlessly stepping on our shadows
or hide behind a curtain
to recite with a stammer the words of the dead
performing the wild joy of the tyrannized

Head for winter
in a land where rivers are frozen
roads begin to flow
on the cobblestones along the river shore
crows hatch out a series of moons
whoever awakens will know
a dream shall befall the earth
precipitating as cold morning frost
replacing the exhausted stars
the time of evil shall come to an end
and icebergs in uninterrupted succession
become a generation's statues

Nightmare

On the shifting wind
I painted an eye
then the blocked moment passed
but no one awoke
the nightmare still overflowed in the sunshine
spilling across the river bed, creeping over the cobbles
provoking new friction and strife
in the branches, on the eaves
the birds' frightened gazes froze into ice
and dropped to earth
then a thin layer of frost
formed over the ruts in the road
no one awoke

The Way Back

The whistle emits an interminable shriek
surely you don't want to keep counting
the crows on the wutong tree
silently memorizing them
as if these signs would prevent you
losing your way in another dream

faded leaves and red buds
sway on the bushes
the wind has actually dropped
but passing by the carriage window
the frost congealed in the dawn light
leaves behind your pale and weary face

yes, in spite of everything
you still want to take the way back
in a place long abandoned
the bamboo pipes of the past
have multiplied into a forest
watching over the road
and sweeping the sky clean

A Toast

The cup is filled with night
without lights, the room floats in its depths
the dotted line along the asphalt road stretches to the
    clouds
without air currents rising; think of
yesterday, searching for peace between lightning flashes
swifts dart in and out of the turret
without being stained by dust
but rows of guns and bouquets
formed a forest and took aim at the lovers' sky
summer is over, and red sorghum
walks along a line of bobbing hats
neither cheerless adulthood nor death
may be averted; the darkness of the night
is so tender in your eyes, yet who
can stop the trains heading for each other in the mist
from colliding at this instant

You Wait for Me in the Rain

You wait for me in the rain
the road leads into the window's depths
the other side of the moon must be very cold
that summer night a white horse
galloped past with the northern lights
for a long time we trembled
go, you said
don't let anger destroy us
leaving no way of escape
like entering the mountain of menopause
at many corners we took the wrong turn
but we met in a desert
all the ages gather here
hawks and long-lived cacti
gather here
more real than heat mirages
as long as one fears birth
and smiling faces that do not don their masks in time
then everything is connected with death
that summer night was not the end
you wait for me in the rain

Résumé

Once I goosestepped across the square
my head shaved bare
the better to seek the sun
but in that season of madness
seeing the cold-faced goats on the other side
of the fence I changed direction
when I saw my ideals
on blank paper like saline-alkaline soil
I bent my spine
believing I had found the only
way to express the truth, like
a baked fish dreaming of the sea
Long live...! I shouted only once, damn it
then sprouted a beard
tangled like countless centuries
I was obliged to do battle with history
and at knife-point formed a
family alliance with idols
not indeed to cope with
the world fragmented in a fly's eye
among piles of endlessly bickering books
calmly we divided into equal shares
the few coins we made from selling off each star
in a single night I gambled away
my belt, and returned naked again to the world
lighting a silent cigarette
it was a gun bringing death at midnight
when heaven and earth changed places
I hung upside down
on an old tree that looked like a mop
gazing into the distance

Rancour turns a drop of water muddy...

Rancour turns a drop of water muddy
I am worn out, the storm
has run aground on the beach
the sun pierced by the mast
is my heart's prisoner, but I
am banished by the world it shines on
nothing is left to sacrifice
on the reef, this dark and pagan altar
except myself, as I go to close or open
the clamorous book

Accomplices

Many years have passed, mica
gleams in the mud
with a bright and evil light
like the sun in a viper's eyes
in a jungle of hands, roads branch off and disappear
where is the young deer
perhaps only a graveyard can change
this wilderness and assemble a town
freedom is nothing but the distance
between the hunter and the hunted
when we turn and look back
the arc drawn by bats
against the vast background of our fathers' portraits
fades with the dusk

we are not guiltless
long ago we became accomplices
of the history in the mirror, waiting for the day
to be deposited in lava
and turn into a cold spring
to meet the darkness once again

Random Thoughts

Dusk rose over the beacon tower
on islands in the border river
a tribe settled
and spread; the land changed colour
myths lay under shabby cotton quilts
the dream's gestation bore poisoned arrows which scattered
painful throbbings; bugles fell silent
skeletons walked at night
unfolding in the wife's unceasing tears
a white screen that blocked
the gate to distant lands

in this piece of amber the east
was a vaguely looming bank
as tufts of reed sped towards the trembling dawn
fishermen quit their boats, and dispersed like the smoke
    from their fires
history, starting out from the bank
felled great thickets of green bamboo
inscribing limited compositions
on imperishable bamboo slips

in the vault a row of ever-burning lamps
witnessed the death of bronze and gold
there is another kind of death
the death of wheat
in the gaps between crossed swords
it grew like a challenge to battle
and set the sun on fire;
the ashes covered winter
cartwheels fell off
scattering in the direction of the spokes

the moat invaded by a dust-storm
is another kind of death; steles
wrapped in moss soft as silk
are like extinguished lanterns

only the road is still alive
the road which outlines the earth's first contours
passing through the endless zone of death
it has reached my feet, stirring up the dust
in the air above the ancient fort puffs of gunsmoke have not
    dispersed
long ago I was cast, but within the ice-cold iron
an impulse is preserved, to call up
the thunder, to call up our ancestors returning from the
    storm
yet if a million souls beneath the earth
should grow into a tall and lonely tree
to shade us, let us taste the bitter fruit
at this time of our departure

The Host

The neglected guest has gone
he left behind news of disaster
and a glove
in order to come knocking at my door again
there's still no way for me to see daylight fireworks
a dance tune strikes up
the moonlight streaming from the mill
is filled with hints of a dream
let us have faith in miracles
a miracle is that nail on the wall
my shadow is trying on
the clothes dangling from the nail
and my last chance at luck
propping up sleep my hands fall
between the two knocks on the door
the dangerous stairs
are outlined against the night

For Many Years

This is you, this is
you, pressed upon by fleeting
shadows, now bright, now dark
no longer shall I go towards you
the cold also makes me despair
for many years, before the icebergs were formed
fish floated up to the water's surface
and sank down, for many years
stepping warily I
passed through the slowly drifting night
lamps glowed on the forked steel prongs
for many years, lonely is
the room without a clock
the people who left may also have taken
the key, for many years
the train on the bridge rushed past
whistling through the fog
season after season
set out from the small station among the fields
paused briefly for every tree
flowered and bore fruit, for many years

Portrait of a Young Poet

The inspiration drawn from your sleeve
is never-ending; you
pass day and night through strung-out lines and
lanes; you
were old when you were born
even though ambition grows as ever
around the edges of your baldness
taking out your false teeth, you
look even more childish
as soon as one's back is turned you scribble your name
on a public lavatory wall
thanks to a poor constitution, you
have to swallow several hormone pills a day
making your voice as tender
as the cat next door in heat
nine sneezes in a row
drop on paper, you
don't mind repetition
saying again that money isn't clean
but everyone is pretty keen on it
a fire engine wails insanely
reminding you to praise
the moon which has paid its insurance premium
or praise the ponderously heavy
axe which hasn't
the axe which weighs more than thought
the weather is mortally cold; blood
darkens, numb
is the night
like a frost-bitten toe, you
limp
in and out of the brake beside the road
meeting laurel-wreathed louts

every tree
with its own owl
running into people you know is a pain
how they do like to bring up the past
the past, yes, you and me
skunks, all of us

The Echo

You can't get out of this valley
in the funeral procession
you can't let go of the coffin by yourself
make peace with death, or let the autumn
continue to stay at home
stay in the tin can beside the stove
and bear infertile buds
the avalanche has started—
the echo seeks the psychological connections.
between you and others: good fortune
lasts, good fortune lasts until tomorrow
but joins tomorrow's
sunbeam, coming from
a jewel hidden in your breast
an evil jewel
you can't get out of this valley, because
the funeral is yours

The Window on the Cliff

From a precarious position the wasp forces open the flower
the letter has been sent, one day in a year
matches, affected by damp, don't shed their light on me any
    more
wolf packs roam among people turned into trees
snowdrifts suddenly thaw; on the dial
winter's silence is intermittent
what bores through the rock is not clean water
chimney-smoke cut by an axe
stands straight up in the air
the sunlight's tiger-skin stripes slip down the wall
stones grow, dreams have no direction
life, scattered amid the undergrowth
ascends in search of a language; stars
shatter; the river on heat
dashes rusty shrapnel towards the city
from sewer ditches hazardous bushes grow
in the markets women buy up spring

Strangers

On the museum's
marble floor, you
took a bad fall, a shoe
slid over the ice-locked river
into the distance, I sat on the table
feeling seasick, endlessly
dialling, not knowing who
I was calling, the stop-work bell
rang three times, following
the silent crowd you gazed
hopelessly at the red light
sunset in a tropical rain forest
is enthralling, I turned the glove
inside out like a banana skin
shaking out sand and loose tobacco
I shaved off my lonely beard again
and together with the soap foam
spattered the dull
mirror, you stepped across the puddle
seeing the stranger's figure
behind was a billboard sky
a glass dove
fell on the floor, I
crawled under the bed in search
my hand was scratched by the gleaming stars
sucking on a lolly
in the dim cinema
you wept over the sad
tale, I switched on the light
and laughed, leaning against the door
with so many chances to get to know you
it would seem we're
not strangers, the door knob
has turned a little

Notes in the Rain

Waking up, the window overlooking the street
preserves the glass pane's
complete and tranquil anguish
gradually turning transparent in the rain
the morning reads my wrinkles
the book lying open on the table
makes a rustling noise, like
the sound of a fire
or fan-like wings
gorgeously opening, flame and bird together
in the space above the abyss

here, between me
and the sunset clouds which herald immutable fate
is a river full of drifting stones
jostling shadows
plunge into its depths
and rising bubbles
menace the starless
daylight

people who draw fruit in the earth
are destined to endure hunger
people who shelter among friends
are destined to be alone
from tree roots exposed beyond life and death
rain water washes away
mud and grass
and the sound of grief

On Tradition

The mountain goat stands on the precipice
the arched bridge decrepit
from the day it was built
who can make out the horizon
through years as dense as porcupines
day and night, windchimes
as sombre
as tattooed men, do not hear ancestral voices
the long night silently enters the stone
the wish to move the stone
is a mountain range rising and falling in history books

Part Three

The August Sleepwalker

the stone bell tolls on the seabed
its tolling stirs up the waves

it is august that tolls
there is no sun at high noon in august

a triangular sail swollen with milk
soars over a drifting corpse

it is august that soars
august apples tumble down the ridge

the lighthouse that died long ago
shines in the seamen's gaze

it is august that shines
the august fair comes close on first frost

the stone bell tolls on the seabed
its tolling stirs up the waves

the august sleepwalker
has seen the sun in the night

One Step

the pagoda's shadow moves across the grass, pointing at
    you
or at me, at different moments
we are only one step away
parting or meeting again
is an ever-repeating
theme: hate only one step away
the sky sways on its foundation of fear
the buildings open windows in every direction
we live inside them
or outside: death only one step away
the child has learned to talk to walls
the history of the city is sealed by old men
in their hearts: dotage only one step away

Another Legend

dead heroes are forgotten
they are lonely, they
pass through a sea of faces
their anger can only light
the cigarette in a man's hand
even with the help of a ladder
they can no longer predict anything
each weather vane goes its own way
only when they huddle
at the foot of their hollow statues
do they realize the depth of despair
they always come and go at night
suddenly illuminated by a single lamp
but difficult to distinguish nonetheless
like faces pressed against frosted glass

finally, they slip through the narrow gate
covered over with dust
taking charge of the solitary key

It has always been so…

it has always been so
that fire is the centre of winter
when the woods are ablaze
only stones that don't want to come closer
keep up their furious howl

the bell hanging on the deer's antlers has stopped ringing
life is one opportunity
a single one only
whoever checks the time
will find himself suddenly old

Temptation

from time immemorial
it has been a temptation
luring sailors to surrender their lives
an embankment preventing
the tilted land from slipping under the sea

a dolphin leapt over the stars
and fell back, the white beach
disappeared in the ample moonlight
seawater covered the embankment
and the empty square
jellyfish clung stranded to every lamp-post
seawater mounted the steps
and poured booming through doors and windows
chasing the man who was dreaming of the sea

Underground Station

these cement electricity poles
were once logs of wood
drifting downriver
do you believe it?
eagles never fly here
though rabbitskin hats of every size and shape
are exposed in the street
do you believe it?
only at night when all is still
flocks of goats pour into town
dyed bright colours by neon lights
do you believe it?

Blanks

poverty is a blank
freedom is a blank
in the sockets of a marble statue
victory is a blank
black birds pouring from the horizon
reveal tomorrow's age spots
despair is a blank
at the bottom of a friend's cup
betrayal is a blank
on the lover's photograph
disgust is a blank
in the long-awaited letter
time is a blank
a swarm of ominous flies
settle on the hospital ceiling
history is a blank
a running genealogy
where only the dead are recognized

A perpetual stranger ...

a perpetual stranger
am I to the world
I don't understand its language
my silence it can't comprehend
all we have to exchange
is a touch of contempt
as if we meet in a mirror

a perpetual stranger
am I to myself
I fear the dark
but block with my body
the only lamp
my shadow is my beloved
heart the enemy

Orphans

we are two orphans
who have made a home
and may leave another orphan behind
in the lengthy
file of orphans trailing pale shadows
all the strident flowers
will bear fruit
this world will know no peace
the earth's wings scatter and fall
the orphans fly to the sky

Bodhisattva

the flowing folds of your robe
are your faint respiration

an unblinking eye stares
on each palm of your thousand arms
they caress the static silence
making all things perpetually intermingle
like dreams

enduring centuries of hunger and thirst
the pearl set in your forehead
stands for the sea's matchless power
that renders a pebble as transparent
as water

your sexless
half-naked bosom swells
it is only a yearning for motherhood
to feed the sufferings of this mortal world
making them grow

The Art of Poetry

in the great house to which I belong
only a table remains, surrounded
by boundless marshland
the moon shines on me from different corners
the skeleton's fragile dream still stands
in the distance, like an undismantled scaffold
and there are muddy footprints on the blank paper
the fox which has been fed for many years
with a flick of his fiery brush flatters and wounds me

and there is you, of course, sitting facing me
the fair-weather lightning which gleams in your palm
turns into firewood turns into ash

Dirge

before the idol, the widow makes an offering
of splintered tears; hungry wolfcubs
are waiting for mother's milk
one by one they have fled the line of life and death
heaving peaks pass on my howl
we besiege the farm together

leaving the farm wreathed in smoke
a ring of wild chrysanthemums nodding in the breeze
you walk towards me, small sturdy breasts outthrust
we meet in the fields
wheat growing wildly on granite cliffs
you are the widow, I

the lost, and lost a lifetime's precious longings
we lie together dripping sweat
the bed afloat on the morning river

Doubtful Things

the fugitive passage of history
a woman's enigmatic smile
are our treasures
open to doubt are the delicate
patterns in marble
signal lights in three colours
stand for the order of the seasons
the man who watches his birdcage
also watches his own age
open to doubt is the small
inn's red roof
the quicksilver of language
drips from a mossy tongue
rushing in all directions
along the flyover bridge
open to doubt is the silent
piano in the apartment building
the small trees in the asylum
are trussed again and again
the model in the shop window
measures shoppers with her glass eyes
open to doubt are bare
feet on the doorstep
open to doubt is our love

Starting from Yesterday

I cannot enter the music
only lower myself to revolve on the black record
to revolve in a blurred moment of time
in the background fixed by lightning
yesterday a subtle fragrance drifted from each flower
yesterday the folding chairs were opened one by one
giving everyone a seat
the sick have been waiting too long
the winter shore in their eyes
stretches further and further away

I can only enter the winter shore
or else the hinterland
sending red leaves scattering in fright
I can only enter the dim school corridors
confronting specimens of every species of bird

The Fable

he lives in his fable
he is no longer the master of the fable
the fable has been resold
into another plump hand

he lives in the plump hand
a canary is his soul
his throat is in a jeweller's shop
around him a glass cage

he lives in the glass cage
between the hats and the shoes
the pocket of the four seasons
is stuffed with a dozen faces

he lives in the twelve faces
but the river he has betrayed
follows closely behind him
recalling the eyes of a dog

he lives in the dog's eyes
he sees the world's hunger
and the wealth of one man
he is the master of his fable

In the Dawn's Bronze Mirror

dawn is displayed
in the dawn's bronze mirror
falcons gather at a single focus
the typhoon's eye is still
where singers cluster on the shore
there is only a hospital, frozen into jade
chanting low

dawn is displayed
in the dawn's bronze mirror
from the patience of despair seamen
know the happiness of stone
and the happiness of the sky
and the happiness of oyster shells that store
a tiny grain of sand

dawn is displayed
in the dawn's bronze mirror
the sail on the roof hasn't yet been hoisted
the grain in the wood unfolds the shapes of the sea
we gaze at each other across the table
and will finally lose
the only dawn between us

Expectation

no long flights of stairs
lead to the loneliest place
no people from different ages
walk on the same whip
no tame deer
roam the wilderness of dreams
there is no expectation

there is only a petrified seed

even the mountain range's lies
do not deny its existence
but the teeth which represent
human wisdom and violence
are waiting in patience
waiting for the single fruit
after the flower's glitter

they have waited several thousand years

the plaza of longing unfolds
unwritten history
a blind man gropes his way
my hand moves over
the blank paper, leaving nothing behind
I am moving
I am the blind man

Electric Shock

I once shook hands with
an invisible man, a cry of pain
a brand was left
on my burning hand
when I shake hands with
visible men, a cry of pain
and a brand is left
on their burning hands
now I dare not shake hands
but hide my hands behind my back
yet when I pray
to heaven, palms pressed together
a cry of pain
and a brand is left
deep in my heart

Language

many languages
fly around the world
producing sparks when they collide
sometimes of hate
sometimes of love

reason's mansion
collapses without a sound
baskets woven of thoughts
as flimsy as bamboo splints
are filled with blind toadstools

the beasts on the cliff
run past, trampling the flowers
a dandelion grows secretly
in a certain corner
the wind has carried away its seeds

many languages
fly around the world
the production of languages
can neither increase nor decrease
mankind's silent suffering

A Single Room

when he was born the furniture was tall and grand
now it is low and shabby
there are no windows or doors, a bulb the only source of
    light
he is content with the room temperature
but curses loudly the bad weather he can't see
hostile bottles stand open-topped in a row
against the wall, his drinking partner unknown
strenuously he hammers nails into the walls
to let an imaginary lame horse surmount these obstacles

a slipper chasing bedbugs tramples
the ceiling, leaving behind prints of patterned ideals
he longs to see blood
his own blood, splashed like the sunset

SOS

rain beats against the dusk
the sharks of unclear nationality
have beached themselves, war bulletins
are still the news
you carry a measuring cup to the sea
grief lies on the sea

in the theatre, the lights dim
you sit among the
finely sculptured ears
you sit in the centre of the noise
and then you go deaf
you have heard the SOS

Deathwatch Night

the small village and all its skinny donkeys
are tethered by withered trees
the roads of the epidemic crisscross
running towards other districts
a century's dust covers the sky

the deathwatch monk only faces
things which have never happened

drifting snowbanks
crowd round the fire in the vicious dog's eyes
the window paper has diffused the weight of the moonlight
the door is quietly pushed open
a century's nights are so graceful

the deathwatch monk only faces
things which have never happened

the padlock rattles and bangs
the wooden box hoards the hours of darkness
the old cat sleeps in a stupor
a mask to ward off evil hangs on the wall
a century's dreams light the oil lamp

the deathwatch monk only faces
things which have never happened

the shrine to the local god at the village entrance
is wreathed in blue smoke
the epitaph gives the stone life
and painless moans
a century's memories arrange swarms of ants

the deathwatch monk only faces
things which have never happened

Space

the children sit in a circle
above a winding valley
not knowing what is below

a memorial column
in the town square
black rain
streets empty of man
sewers leading to another
town

we sit in a circle
around a dead stove
not knowing what is above

Don't Ask Our Ages

in an innocent forest and on a flying carpet
of grass we have approached the sky

when we occupied a certain apartment house
as one occupies the truth
the bus mistakenly entered the city network
and climbed up the concrete precipice
among houses bound in electric wires
night brought a letter from a stranger
the staircase went limp
the stone lion caught in the trap
is our common master

don't ask our ages
like fish in cold storage we are fast asleep
our false teeth lie in a cup
our shadows have cast us off
cut once again
a withered branch growing from the sleeve
has burst open a row
of blood-red mouths

Daydream

I

after the autumn atrocities
this November, drugged by ice and frost
flattens on the wall
shadow upon shadow, layer upon layer
it is a process of skeletal petrification
you did not come back at the time as arranged
the kernel in my throat
became a warm stone

I look like a dubious character
the new season's review of troops
knocks on my window
people who live in clocks
run with swaying hearts
I look down on time
not having to turn round
a year's darkness in my cup

II

music liberates a blue soul
drifting over the cigarette tip
in and out of the door and window cracks

an apple ready for slicing
—there is no kernel
no seed to grow hostility

far away from the magnetic field of the sun
hair that has grown in the glasshouse
is like seaweed, avoiding true

storms, we are
children lost in an airport

wanting to burst into tears

in cinemascopic disturbances
noses absorbing dust
bump into each other
talking without stopping: this is I
I
I, we

            III

books, murmuring in dreams
line up in rows
waiting at three a.m.
for heterodox flames

time is not tormented
we have deserted mountain forests and lakes
gathering together
why are we together
a tin crow
sits on a marble pedestal
the welded seams of things which are eternal
will not crack

people awakening from inside stone coffins
sit with me
our group photograph, we and the epoch together
hangs at the end of the long table

            IV

you did not come back at the time as arranged
and herein lies the point of our parting
one tour of love
is sometimes as simple
as smoking a cigarette

the cellar is reserved for your
heart's pure silver
a narcissus blooms bright in the dark
you let all the bad weather
grow angry, weep and howl
begging you to open the window

the pages turn
the writing scatters
leaving behind only a number
—the number of my seat
next to the window
the train's terminus is you

V

the sunflower's cap flies away without wings
the stone is smooth and reliable
preserving the integrity of the essence
in a place where no people dwell
even the mountains become young
the evening bell does not necessarily explain anything
giant pythons evolve by sloughing off skin
ropes tie knots
and hang up fish
a pool of dead water summons innumerable lightning
    flashes
tigers' and leopards' spots and stripes gradually turn blue
the sky has been swallowed

history is silent
cliffs gaze after the child
on the river who has drifted down from the source
this child of humanity

VI

I need a public square
an empty square
to set out a bowl, a small spoon
and the lonely shadow of a kite

the people occupying the square say
it's not possible

a bird in a cage needs a walk
a sleepwalker needs anaemic sunshine
paths in collision
need a dialogue between equals

people's impulses have condensed into
uranium stored in a safe place

in a small shop
a banknote, a razor blade
and a packet of extra-strength insecticide
are born

VII

the year I died I was ten years old
the ball I cast into the air never
fell to the ground
you were the only eyewitness
at ten, I knew
afterwards I climbed aboard
the train transporting buffaloes
I am listed in the expired bill of lading
for people to read

this morning
a bird flew through my open newspaper
your face is framed in it

a passion that has lasted a long time
still gleams in the depths of your eyes
I will forever dwell in
the shadow that you designed

VIII

for many years
many refugees from the fire
blocked the light of the sun and moon
the white horse unfolded a long bandage
the wooden stake pierced the coal seam
dark red blood oozes out
the poisonous spider plucks its strings
dropping from the sky
on open ground, fire-balls roll to and fro

for many years
many rivers dried up
exposing what was secret
it is an empty, bare museum
whoever places himself within it
may regard himself as an exhibit
to be gazed at by invisible glances
just like an insect asleep for a thousand years
released by the amber's explosion

IX

finally one day
people as fearless as lies
walked out from the outsize radio
praising disaster'
the doctor raised a white sheet
standing on a sick tree he shouted:
it's freedom, unvaccinated freedom
that has poisoned you

only sound exists
a few simple, feeble sounds
like parthenogenic organisms
they are the lawful heirs
of the inscription on the ancient bell
heroes, clowns, politicians
and women with slender ankles
hide among the sounds

X

hands gasp
tassels moan
carved lattices interlock
a paper lantern passes along the verandah
at the far end it is extinguished
an arrow strikes the palace gate

memorial tablets topple in succession
—nightmares in a chain reaction
sons and grandsons
are rotten teeth
in the mouths of stately stone lions

the courtyard which locked in the scenery those years
has only a single tree left
they dance around the tree
constraints all forgotten in drunkenness
madness is an exception

XI

don't take your lust into autumn
this cripple's autumn
loudly whistling autumn

a woman's dry hand
brushes across the sea but doesn't touch one drop of water
the evening sunset cloud which moves reefs
is your lust
setting me on fire

heart like a dry well
my desire for the sea drew me away from the sea
walking towards my beginning—you
or towards your ending—me

in the end we'll be lost in the fog
calling to each other
from different places
becoming useless road signs

XII

a long white gown floats towards that
place which doesn't exist
heart like a water-pump throbbing in a summer night
for no reason pours out its feelings
the twilight banquet is over
the mountain ranges disperse
mayflies write poems on the water
the odes of the horizon stop and start
a shadow is never a man's history
masks are doffed or donned
flowers are born of necessity
lies and grief are inseparable
if there are no masks
how can clocks still have meaning

when souls display their true form in rock
only a bird can recognize them

XIII

pointing out a silvery marsh he said
there a battle took place
smoking trees raced along the horizon
soldiers and horses that had gone underground
glowed phosphorescent, day and night
they followed the general's armour

but what we followed after was
the animal skin free and in flight
among stray bullets of ideology

the heads of those who died in the battles of those days
rose up like the moon in the last quarter
soaring over the rustling bushes
saying in the tone of a prophet
you are in no way survivors
you will never have a home

a new ideology whistled past
it hit the back of the age
a drop of fly's blood stunned me

XIV

I am destined to sit on the river bank
on a piece of blank paper
awaiting words, like old-age spots

to appear in order and in confusion
honeycomb cells manufacture different lusts
ninety-nine red mountain peaks

ascend, the atmosphere is thin
lichen, with evil intent, spreads
triviality, like this world's

schemes, their power supported by reinforcing rods
even stones can get dizzy
it is in the end a terrible

height, behind the blank paper
a child's hand plays shadow games
the light comes from a pair of copulating eels
at the bottom of the sea

XV

night squatting in the earthenware jar
spilt cool clear
water, the source of our love

memory is like a scar
my whole life was at your feet
the shifting sand-dune
fused in your hand
into a glittering diamond

without a bed, the room
was so small we could not part
the four walls thin as tissue paper
innumerable mouths drawn on the walls
singing rounds in low voices

you did not get back at the time as arranged
the cup that we drank from
together cracks

XVI

the mine was abandoned long ago
its metal drawn out into thin long wire

light shines through the owl's body
stomach and nerve clusters sweep over the night sky

the alliance of palaeo-organisms has dissolved
the task of sticking fossils together

is still underway, existence
is forever a collective adventure

existence forever undertakes
war with spring

green caterpillar-treads have crushed
a dreary civilization

the metal head of a sprinkler spraying
mercury has changed the landform

at peace, dreamless

XVII

several centuries have passed
one day has not yet started
cold air has touched my hand
rising like a spiral staircase
black and white, rays of light
on the musical scale of the roof-tiles have metamorphosed
into the tranquillity of a date tree
men's throats have ripened

the cornered beasts in the zoo
are enclosed in a row of books
a steel whip twirls
brilliant palpitating colours
separated by endless long years
are wailing bitterly
a tourist map leads me
into a city within a city
stars are crafty and cruel
like the kernel of an event

XVIII

I am always strolling
along the street's lonely will
oh, my city slides
on glassy solid ice

my city my story
my watertap my grievances
my parrot my
sleep that preserves equilibrium

the young woman whose scent is like poppies
floats by from the supermarket
people with expressions like penknives
drink the winter sun's cold light together

poetry like a balcony
tortures me without mercy
walls plastered with grime
are not unexpected

XIX

when you turn around
granite bursts and cracks into fine quicksand
you speak in an unfamiliar tone
to emptiness, as false
as the smile on your face

the bitter roots planted deep in yesterday
are lightning flashes in darkest places
beating against our imagination's nest
in the trickle of quicksand
we hear the music of crystals colliding

a minor surgical operation
on the snowy ground where we excavated flintstones
are tracks left by sparrows
a wild winter cart
passes through summer's flames

we are safe and sound
beautiful scenes from four seasons
are painted on your clothing

XX

herding is a statement of viewpoint
a heat illness makes the sheep swell
like a trail of rising balloons
stuck in Scorpio
the hot wind rolls away my roof
inside the four walls
I sit still and gaze at the sky without writing
culture is a symbiotic phenomenon
which includes the value of sheep
and the morality of wolves
there is nothing inside the clock cover
within our field of vision
there is only a dried up river bed
and a few straight wisps of smoke
the sages of ancient days
in infinite loneliness
spend their time fishing

XXI

secretive peapods have five eyes
they are not willing to look at the sun
but listen in the dark

a colour is a child's
birth wail

the banquet cloth is pure white
in the cup is a taste of death
—the oppressive smell volatilized by the eulogy

tradition is an aerial photo
landscapes reduced to a birch-trunk grain

people are always subservient
to preaching, to imitation, to struggle
and to their own dignity

the traveller who seeks passion
passes through bleak habitats of migratory birds

the plaster statues open the window
from behind, the artist
savagely smashes them with his hammer

XXII

the trumpet made dumb with a mute
suddenly blares forth
the director of the great tragedy
is dying quietly
two lions installed by pulleys
still dash to and fro
on fixed tracks

the first light of dawn is paralysed on the main street
a host of addresses and names and cares
shelter from the rain in the pillarbox at night
geese in the goods train yard cackle
the window yawns
on a morning with the smell of lysol
the doctor on duty fills in the death report

the great significance of this tragedy, ah
the trivial details of daily life

XXIII

a crack has appeared between day and night

language suddenly becomes stale
like the first fall of snow
the witnesses who hid their faces with black cloth
pressed around you
you stuck a row of pine branches in the ground
and silently set them alight

it was a funeral ceremony rite
on death's mountain ridge
I occupied a commanding position
who are you
what do you want to exchange with me
the white crane unfolds a sheet of drifting paper
on it is written your answer
but I know nothing at all

you did not come back at the time as arranged
the cup that we drank from
together cracks

Frédéric Mistral, *The Memoirs*. NDP632.
Eugenio Montale, *It Depends*.† NDP507.
  Selected Poems.† NDP193.
Paul Morand, *Fancy Goods / Open All Night*. NDP567.
Vladimir Nabokov, *Nikolai Gogol*. NDP78.
  Laughter in the Dark. NDP470.
  The Real Life of Sebastian Knight. NDP432.
P. Neruda, *The Captain's Verses*.† NDP345.
  Residence on Earth.† NDP340.
New Directions in Prose & Poetry (Anthology).
  Available from #50 forward to #54.
Robert Nichols, *Arrival*. NDP437.
  Exile. NDP485. *Garh City*. NDP450.
  Harditts in Sawna. NDP470.
J. F. Nims, *The Six-Cornered Snowflake*. NDP700.
Charles Olson, *Selected Writings*. NDP231.
Toby Olson, *The Life of Jesus*. NDP417.
  Seaview. NDP532.
George Oppen, *Collected Poems*. NDP418.
István Örkeny, *The Flower Show / The Toth Family*.
  NDP536.
Wilfred Owen, *Collected Poems*. NDP210.
José Emilio Pacheco, *Battles in the Desert*. NDP637.
  Selected Poems.† NDP638.
Nicanor Parra, *Antipoems: New & Selected*. NDP603.
Boris Pasternak, *Safe Conduct*. NDP77.
Kenneth Patchen, *Aflame and Afun*. NDP292.
  Because It Is. NDP83.
  Collected Poems. NDP284.
  Selected Poems. NDP160.
Octavio Paz, *Configurations*.† NDP303.
  A Draft of Shadows.† NDP489.
  Eagle or Sun?† NDP422.
  Selected Poems. NDP574.
  A Tree Within.† NDP661.
St. John Perse, *Selected Poems*.† NDP545.
J. A. Porter, *Eelgrass*. NDP438.
Ezra Pound, *ABC of Reading*. NDP89.
  Confucius. NDP285.
  Confucius to Cummings. (Anth.) NDP126.
  A Draft of XXX Cantos. NDP690.
  Elektra. NDP683.
  Gaudier Brzeska. NDP372.
  Guide to Kulchur. NDP257.
  Literary Essays. NDP250.
  Selected Cantos. NDP304.
  Selected Letters 1907-1941. NDP317.
  Selected Poems. NDP66.
  The Spirit of Romance. NDP266.
  Translations.† (Enlarged Edition) NDP145.
Raymond Queneau, *The Blue Flowers*. NDP595.
  Exercises in Style. NDP513.
  The Flight of Icarus. NDP358.
Mary de Rachewiltz, *Ezra Pound*. NDP405.
Raja Rao, *Kanthapura*. NDP224.
Herbert Read, *The Green Child*. NDP208.
P. Reverdy, *Selected Poems*.† NDP346.
Kenneth Rexroth, *Classics Revisited*. NDP621.
  More Classics Revisited. NDP668.
  100 More Poems from the Chinese. NDP308.
  100 More Poems from the Japanese.† NDP420.
  100 Poems from the Chinese. NDP192.
  100 Poems from the Japanese.† NDP147.
  Selected Poems. NDP581.
  Women Poets of China. NDP528.
  Women Poets of Japan. NDP527.
  World Outside the Window, Sel. Essays. NDP639.
Rainer Maria Rilke, *Poems from The Book of Hours*.
  NDP408.
  Possibility of Being. (Poems). NDP436.
  Where Silence Reigns. (Prose). NDP464.
Arthur Rimbaud, *Illuminations*.† NDP56.
  Season in Hell & Drunken Boat.† NDP97.
Edouard Roditi, *Delights of Turkey*. NDP445.
  Oscar Wilde. NDP624.
Jerome Rothenberg, *Khurbn*. NDP679.
  New Selected Poems. NDP625.
Nayantara Sahgal, *Rich Like Us*. NDP665.

Ihara Saikaku, *The Life of an Amorous Woman*.
  NDP270.
St. John of the Cross, *Poems*.† NDP341.
William Saroyan, *Madness in the Family*. NDP691.
Jean-Paul Sartre, *Nausea*. NDP82.
  The Wall (Intimacy). NDP272.
Peter Dale Scott, *Coming to Jakarta*. NDP672.
Delmore Schwartz, *Selected Poems*. NDP241.
  The Ego Is Always at the Wheel. NDP641.
  In Dreams Begin Responsibilities. NDP454.
  Last & Lost Poems. NDP673.
Shattan, *Manimekhalai*. NDP674.
Stevie Smith, *Collected Poems*. NDP562.
  New Selected Poems. NDP659.
  Some Are More Human. . . . NDP680.
Gary Snyder, *The Back Country*. NDP249.
  The Real Work. NDP499.
  Regarding Wave. NDP306.
  Turtle Island. NDP381.
G. Sobin, *Voyaging Portraits*. NDP651.
Enid Starkie, *Rimbaud*. NDP254.
Robert Steiner, *Bathers*. NDP495.
Antonio Tabucchi, *Letter from Casablanca*. NDP620
  Little Misunderstandings. . . . NDP681.
Dylan Thomas, *Adventures in the Skin Trade*. NDP18
  A Child's Christmas in Wales. NDP181.
  Collected Poems 1934-1952. NDP316.
  Collected Stories. NDP626.
  Portrait of the Artist as a Young Dog. NDP51.
  Quite Early One Morning. NDP90.
  Under Milk Wood. NDP73.
Tian Wen: *A Chinese Book of Origins*. NDP624.
Uwe Timm, *The Snake Tree*. NDP686.
Niccolo Tucci, *The Rain Came Last*. NDP688.
Tu Fu, *Selected Poems*. NDP675.
Lionel Trilling, *E. M. Forster*. NDP189.
Martin Turnell, *Baudelaire*. NDP336.
Paul Valéry, *Selected Writings*.† NDP184.
Elio Vittorini, *A Vittorini Omnibus*. NDP366.
Rosmarie Waldrop, *The Reproduction of Profiles*.
  NDP649.
Robert Penn Warren, *At Heaven's Gate*. NDP588.
Vernon Watkins, *Selected Poems*. NDP221.
Eliot Weinberger, *Works on Paper*. NDP627.
Nathanael West, *Miss Lonelyhearts & Day of the Locus*
  NDP125.
J. Wheelwright, *Collected Poems*. NDP544.
Tennessee Williams, *Camino Real*. NDP301.
  Cat on a Hot Tin Roof. NDP398.
  Clothes for a Summer Hotel. NDP556.
  The Glass Menagerie. NDP218.
  Hard Candy. NDP225.
  In the Winter of Cities. NDP154.
  A Lovely Sunday for Creve Coeur. NDP497.
  One Arm & Other Stories. NDP237.
  Red Devil Battery Sign. NDP650.
  A Streetcar Named Desire. NDP501.
  Sweet Bird of Youth. NDP409.
  Twenty-Seven Wagons Full of Cotton. NDP217.
  Vieux Carre. NDP482.
William Carlos Williams,
  The Autobiography. NDP223.
  The Buildup. NDP259.
  The Doctor Stories. NDP585.
  Imaginations. NDP329.
  In the American Grain. NDP53.
  In the Money. NDP240.
  Paterson. Complete. NDP152.
  Pictures from Brueghel. NDP118.
  Selected Poems (new ed.). NDP602.
  White Mule. NDP226.
  Yes, Mrs. Williams. NDP534.
Yvor Winters, *E. A. Robinson*. NDP326.
Wisdom Books: Early Buddhists. NDP444; *Spanish
  Mystics*. NDP442; *St. Francis*. NDP477; *Taoists*.
  NDP509; *Wisdom of the Desert*. NDP295; *Zen
  Masters*. NDP415.

For complete listing request free catalog from
New Directions, 80 Eighth Avenue, New York 10011

†Bilingual